WORKING WITH
STAINED GLASS

PAUL W. WOOD

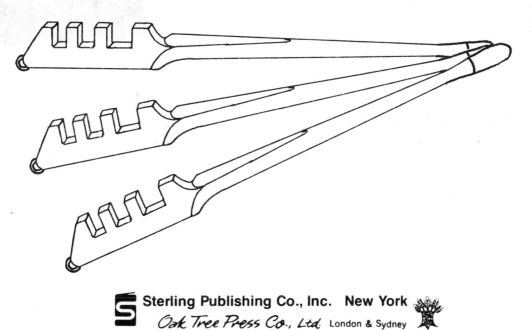

Sterling Publishing Co., Inc.   New York
Oak Tree Press Co., Ltd. London & Sydney

To my wife, Jacqueline, whose loving support and understanding made this book possible.

ACKNOWLEDGMENTS

The author wishes especially to thank Mr. Burton Hobson not only for his invaluable advice and assistance in preparing the text of this book but also for the photographs both black and white and color which illustrate and explain it.

Thanks are also due to my younger son Paul for his artistry and assistance in the creation of the stained glass projects.

Metric Conversion Chart

$\frac{1}{8}$ inch = 3.18 millimetres	$\frac{5}{8}$ inch = 15.88 millimetres	$1\frac{1}{2}$ inch = 38.10 millimetres
$\frac{1}{4}$ inch = 6.35 millimetres	$\frac{3}{4}$ inch = 19.05 millimetres	2 inches = 50.80 millimetres
$\frac{3}{8}$ inch = 9.53 millimetres	$\frac{7}{8}$ inch = 22.23 millimetres	1 foot = 30.48 centimetres
$\frac{1}{2}$ inch = 12.70 millimetres	1 inch = 25.40 millimetres	1 yard = 0.9144 metre
	10 millimetres = 1 centimetre	

Styrofoam® is a trademark of Dow Chemical Company.

"Working with Stained Glass"
Copyright © 1981 by Sterling Publishing Co., Inc.
Two Park Avenue, New York, N.Y. 10016
is based on
"Artistry in Stained Glass"
© 1976 by Sterling Publishing Co., Inc. and
"Starting with Stained Glass"
© 1973 by Sterling Publishing Co., Inc.
Distributed in Australia by Oak Tree Press Co., Ltd.
P.O. Box J34, Brickfield Hill, Sydney 2000, N.S.W.
Distributed in the United Kingdom
by Oak Tree Press Ltd. U.K.
Available in Canada from Oak Tree Press Ltd.
℅ Canadian Manda Group, 215 Lakeshore Boulevard East
Toronto, Ontario M5A 3W9
Manufactured in the United States of America
All rights reserved

Library of Congress Cataloging in Publication Data

Wood, Paul W.
  Working with stained glass.

  Based on the author's Artistry in stained glass and
Starting with stained glass.
  Includes index.
  Summary: A beginner's introduction to the materials,
tools, and techniques for making such stained glass
pieces as pendants, medallions, hanging ornaments,
figurines, candlestick holders, and lamp shades.
  1. Glass craft. [1. Glass painting and staining.
2. Glass craft. 3. Handicraft] I. Title.
TT298.W68 1981   748.5   80-54350
ISBN 0-8069-5440-X   AACR2
ISBN 0-8069-5441-8 (lib. bdg.)
ISBN 0-8069-8966-1 (pbk.)

Contents

    Color section follows page 48.

Before You Begin

New techniques and modern materials make it possible for the craftsman to use traditional stained glass in fresh, creative ways. Originally used primarily for religious windows, stained glass now brings color and light to homes and commercial buildings.

Here in simple, easy-to-follow steps is everything you need to know to work with this jewel-like transparent material. You are introduced directly to the techniques of the craft. The progressively more difficult projects that follow give you a chance to develop your skill and exercise your own creativity.

Materials

Some pieces of stained glass are, of course, the first requirement. If you are near a commercial stained glass workshop, you can probably purchase scrap glass of various types, colors, and textures from them. Many shops also offer small quantities of lead, solder, and other essentials to individual craftsmen. More and more art and craft supply shops are carrying stock of stained glass materials and, in the larger cities, professional stained glass supply houses will handle large orders.

Some craftsmen look for odd pieces of colored glass along the beach or in old trash heaps. You can often fit a piece of an old broken bottle of an interesting color into a project. Louis Tiffany, famous for his lamps, often used pieces of broken bottles, first melting them together in a kiln, to produce his special variegated glass.

Tools

In addition to a few common household tools, you will need only a mat knife or a linoleum knife for cutting the lead came, a glass cutter, a soldering iron and a pair of needle-nosed pliers.

Glass cutters have a small wheel at the tip that does the actual scoring. The different-sized notches are used to break off thin strips or rough pieces of glass.

Cutting Glass

You must have a flat, sturdy table or bench for successful cutting. A piece of old carpet makes a good bench top. To "cut" glass, you first score it with a cutter and then break it along the scored line. If you are using an old cutter, be sure that the wheel is sharp and free of rust. Cutting glass is not difficult, but it does take a little experience before you can be sure of scoring it evenly and breaking it cleanly every time. You may want to make your first practice cuts on some scraps of inexpensive window glass.

Straight-line cuts are the easiest to make, so you will find it best to use rectangular shapes for your first projects. If you do use curved shapes, be sure they are outside curves (convex) and make them as gently sloped as possible. Also try to avoid having to cut pieces less than an inch wide.

Before you start cutting, clean the glass with a damp cloth or piece of fine steel wool. Any dust or film on the surface will cause the cutter wheel to skip. Lay a sheet of colored glass directly over the pattern for the largest piece you will need of

A piece of felt or an old carpet covering the top of a sturdy table provides a good surface for cutting glass.

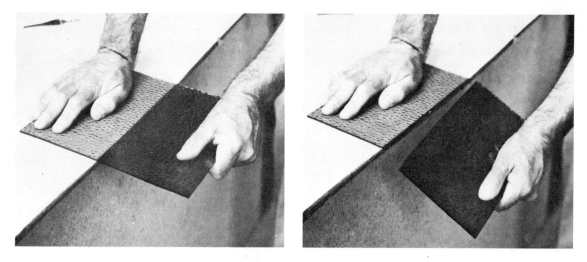

After the glass has been scored, place it parallel to the edge of the table so that the scored line extends slightly beyond the table edge. Snap the projecting piece downwards.

that color. Most stained glass has one side that is smoother than the other. Score the smooth side as the rougher surface will tend to deflect the cutter. Position the glass so as to use the existing edges whenever possible. Wherever you do have to break off glass, leave a margin of at least an inch beyond the edge of the pattern. Now score the glass, following the pattern underneath. Hold the cutter with the wheel pressed downwards against the glass with the notched edge of the cutter towards you. The cutter must be perpendicular to the glass. The ball end of the cutter goes between your first two fingers: use your thumb and index finger to bear down on the shoulders of the cutter. Dip the wheel in kerosene or turpentine occasionally to lubricate it, making your job easier.

Bearing down firmly with the cutter wheel, start at the edge away from you and draw the cutter steadily towards you. Maintain the downwards pressure all the way across. You will find that some pieces of glass are harder than others and you will have to apply more pressure to score them. Don't start or end your cuts at the very edge of the glass, however, to avoid chipping it. Stop and start a small fraction of an inch from the edge. Bear down hard enough so that the scoring shows clearly on the glass. Remember, though, you are only scoring the glass, not trying to cut all the way through it! When the cutter is scoring properly, it makes an even biting or rasping sound. Don't try to go over a line more than once.

Curved shapes must be scored freehand, but you can use a ruler or other straightedge to guide the cutter over straight lines. If you do use a guide, be sure to note that the cutter wheel scores approxi-

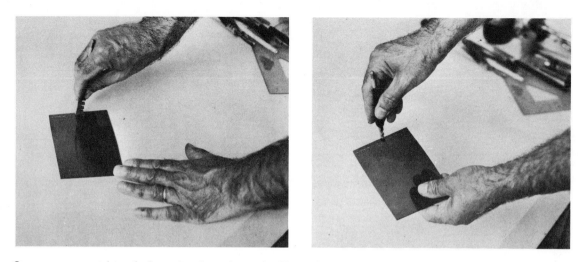

Score narrow strips of glass slowly and evenly. Place the cutter notch in the middle of the thin strip and snap downwards.

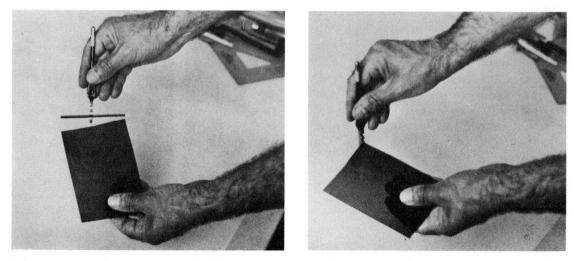

Select the notch in the head of the glass cutter which most nearly matches the thickness of the glass. Use the notched end of the cutter to nibble away uneven protrusions of glass.

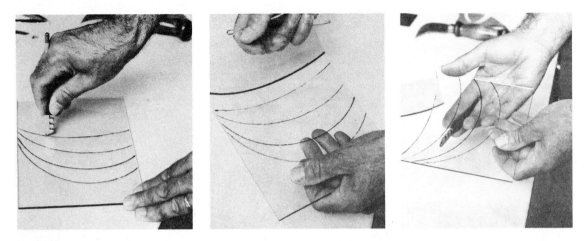

For deeply curved pieces, first score a slight curve, then several progressively deeper ones until the desired curve is scored. Tap out the pieces of glass in the same order as they were scored.

mately $\frac{1}{16}$ inch out from the edge. The cutter may skip around on the smooth surface of the glass at first, but with a little practice you will soon have it under control.

Once the glass is scored, you are ready to break it. If you are breaking the glass along a straight line, and if you have enough glass to hold it firmly on both sides of the line, press the pattern piece flat against the table with one hand so that the scored line is just along or slightly beyond and parallel to the edge of the table. Grasp the excess glass firmly with your hand and snap downwards. If you should have trouble breaking the glass, tap from below with the cutter along the length of the scored line until a crack appears under the line. Tap smartly, but tap, don't hammer. If the piece of glass is fairly small, try gripping it firmly on both sides of the scored line and apply pressure downwards and away from the line until it snaps.

Professional stained glass craftsmen dull the cut edges by scraping the edge of a piece of scrap glass along them. Take the time to dull the edge of each

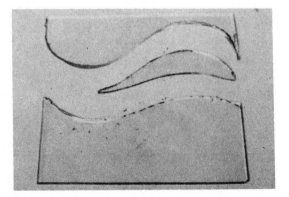

Cut this difficult double curve following the procedure at right.

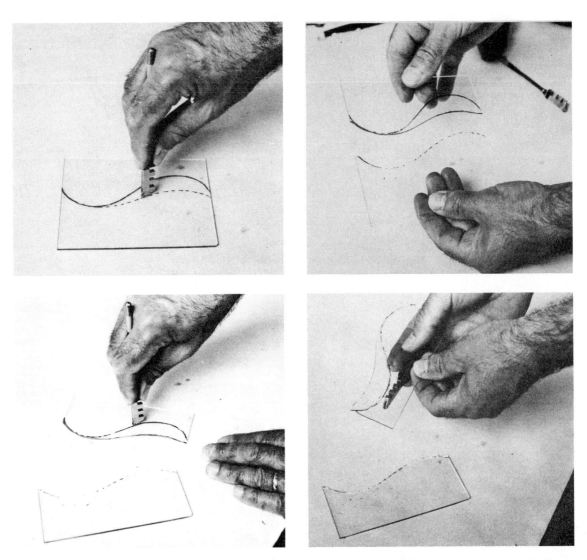

After first drawing the double curve directly on the glass with a soft-tip marker, add an additional dotted line at a lesser curve. Now score along the dotted line and separate the glass. Finally, score the deeper curve and tap under the score line until the small middle piece falls out.

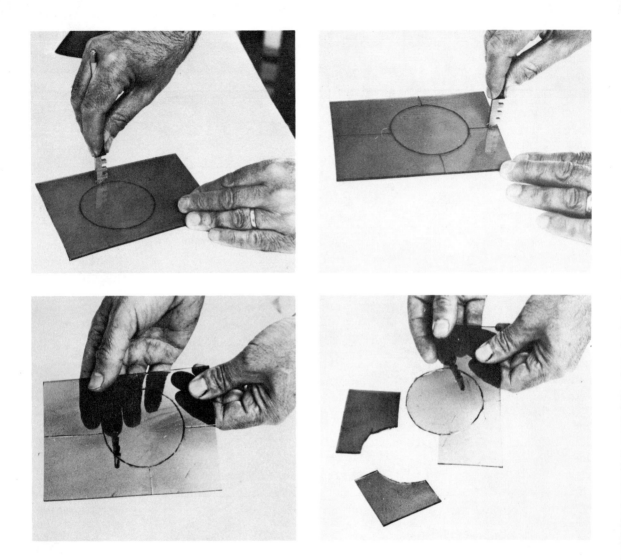

To cut a complete circle of glass, start by scoring the circle itself. Then score four additional lines from the circle to the four edges of the piece of glass. Tap out the wedges one at a time until only the circle is left.

10

Remove any protrusions of glass by grozing them with either the cutter notches or a grozing pliers.

piece of glass as soon as you cut it. Have a scrap box handy for the disposal of small pieces while you are cutting.

To cut off pieces less than an inch wide, score the glass as above, but break it off by tapping. Keep tapping from edge to edge until the glass breaks off along the scored line. Hold the glass close to the surface of your work table so that when the glass piece breaks off it will not fall to the floor and shatter. Caution: don't try to catch the sharp-edged glass. If it misses the table top, let it fall rather than risk a cut. Cut off very narrow pieces by scoring the glass, and then break off the excess, using one of the notches on the side of the glass cutter. Grip the narrow strip of glass in the notch nearest in size to the thickness of the sheet itself.

Score curved cuts in the same manner and break them by tapping. To cut a deep curve, score two additional, more gradual curves next to it. Use your glass cutter to tap out the first curved piece of glass, then the second and the third.

To cut a full circle in glass, carefully score the entire perimeter on a piece of glass that is 2 or 3 inches larger than the diameter of the circle itself. Score four additional lines from the circle to the edge of the glass at each quarter turn. Tap along underneath the circular score a quarter segment at a time, allowing each segment in turn to fall away.

Uneven protrusions of glass along the cut edge can be smoothed off by working away at them with the notched teeth of the cutter. (This is called

11

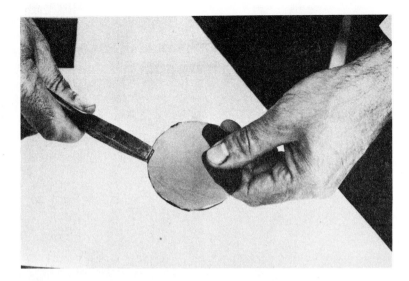

grozing.) Alternatively, you can buy special grozing pliers to smooth off protrusions of glass even more effectively.

With a reasonable amount of care, you can handle, cut, and assemble stained glass with little danger of cutting yourself. Sensible precautions, however, help prevent accidents. Do not put away glass with sharp projections pointing outwards. Throw scraps into a sturdy box, and brush your work surface frequently to clean up any little slivers of glass.

Dull the freshly cut edges of each piece of glass
by scraping with a piece of scrap glass.

A wood frame which holds samples of glass against the light from a window makes color selection easy.

Soldering

Use a medium-size soldering iron rated between 100 and 200 watts. If you have a new iron, the copper tip must be "tinned" (coated with solder) before you can use it. To do this, plug in the iron and bring it up to "hot" (4–5 minutes). Sprinkle some rosin on a flat piece of copper and rub the tip of the iron into the rosin, at the same time holding the solder next to the tip. The solder will flow on, making the tip shiny. While you are

soldering, keep a piece of damp sponge handy and wipe the tip of the iron on it from time to time to keep solder from building up. If, after repeated use, your soldering-iron tip becomes rough and corroded, file it down to the copper base and repeat the procedure.

Soldering is simple if you use the proper solder and flux, a clean soldering-iron tip, and the right heat. The temperature of the soldering iron has to be watched carefully. At the correct heat, a piece of solder held against the tip will melt readily. If the iron becomes too hot it will melt the came or copper foil; if too cool it will not melt the solder. Test your soldering iron on scrap pieces to judge the temperature.

Use solid, no-core solder. The easiest to work with is made up of 60% tin, 40% lead. The first step in actually soldering joints is to use a brush to put a drop or two of flux (oleic acid) at the point where two pieces come together. Now touch the hot iron tip to the joint and simultaneously touch the solder to the tip. The solder will run across the joint, bonding it together. With a little practice, you will learn to use the minimum amount of solder necessary to form a bond, avoiding unsightly big bubbles of solder. Too much solder does not make a stronger joint.

Don't use too short a piece of solder as it will be uncomfortably hot near the iron tip and you unnecessarily run the risk of burning your fingers. Keep your soldering iron unplugged and resting on its metal support when not in use.

The heavy-duty soldering iron shown here can be used for almost any stained-glass project. A soldering gun is useful for spot soldering or when you are soldering only one or two joints at a time. The heat turns off automatically when the trigger is released.

14

Stained Glass Terrarium

The easiest technique for attaching pieces of glass to one another is the copper-foil method. It is especially good for three-dimensional constructions or for flat works that contain intricately shaped pieces of glass.

Choose a relatively light color stained glass with a seedy texture for a terrarium. The light color will let you see the plants clearly as well as allow them to receive sufficient light. The seedy texture gives the glass a distinctive look and creates interesting patterns with the light passing through it.

If this is your first attempt at working with glass, you should plan a terrarium with rectangular sides. Start by drawing a full-size, accurately drawn plan. Use a ruler and exact measurements. Now place a piece of the glass over the design, making use of existing edges wherever possible. Clean the glass by wiping it off with a piece of fine steel wool. Hold a straightedge firmly along the line to be cut, but remember that the wheel scores approximately $\frac{1}{16}$ inch away from the straightedge. Run the cutter smoothly along the guide, scoring the glass directly above the pattern line. A good way to break the glass along these lengthy cuts is to place the scored glass on a table and lay the round end of the cutter under one end of the scored line. Press the glass down on

This simple terrarium makes a dramatic home for your house plants.

Draw an accurate plan for the end and side panels of the terrarium.

each side of the scored line and the glass should break cleanly along the entire cut. Follow the same procedure to cut the remaining sides. Remember to dull the edges by scraping them with a piece of scrap glass.

Before applying the copper foil, be sure the glass edges are clean. Running steel wool around each edge will ensure that the foil will adhere properly. Unroll a small length of copper foil, pulling away the paper backing as you go to uncover the adhe-

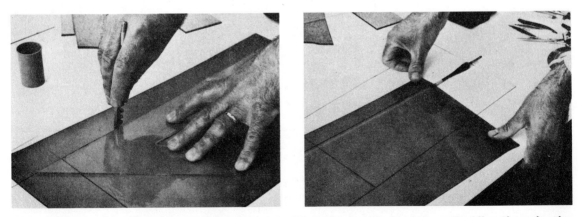

For accuracy use a straightedge to guide the cutter. Place the round end of the cutter directly under the end of the second line. Snap down on both sides of the scored line simultaneously for a perfect cut.

16

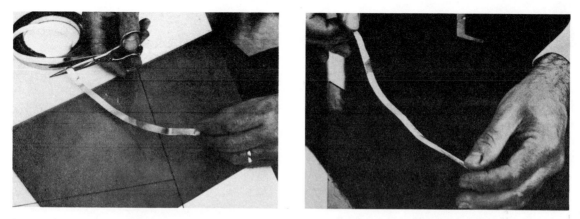

Snip off copper-foil tape, allowing enough length to wrap around the corners. Hook the end of the copper foil at one corner, pulling it evenly while sticking it to the edge of the glass.

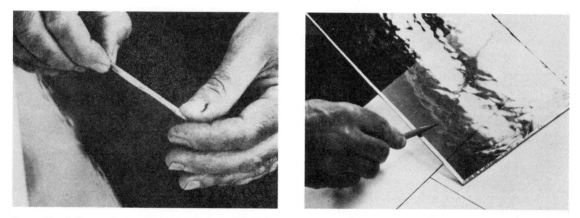

Press the foil evenly around the edge of the glass piece. Smooth down the foil with a pencil or a piece of wood until it adheres tightly to the glass.

sive back of the copper. Begin wrapping the edges of the glass by catching the foil at a corner and unrolling it a few inches at a time along the edge. Press the copper against the glass so that it adheres tightly. Continue wrapping around the four edges of the glass, overlapping the copper tape slightly when you arrive back at your starting point. Bend and fold the foil around onto the face and back of the glass with equal amounts on each side. Smooth the foil down with a wooden pencil or the round

17

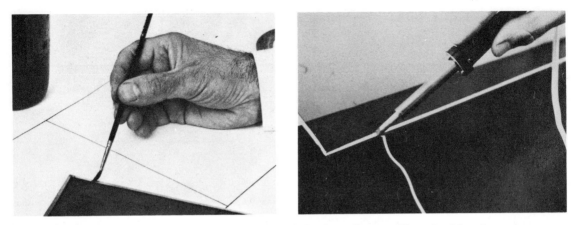

Spread a thin coat of oleic acid flux on the copper foil edges. Draw a film of solder along the copper foil with the tip of the soldering iron.

Hold one side piece and one end piece together with masking tape while spot-soldering the top corner. Repeat the spot-soldering at each top and bottom corner of the terrarium.

end of your glass cutter. Repeat this wrapping procedure with each piece of glass until the edges of all the sides are covered with foil. Now you are ready to cover the foil with a coat of solder to make it rigid.

Brush a light coat of oleic acid flux onto the copper foil so that the solder will flow smoothly over it. Start with a drop of solder at one corner and use the hot soldering iron to pull the solder down over the copper in a smooth film. Continue soldering until all of the sides and edges of the copper are coated with solder. To join the sides together, stand two of them at right angles to one another and spot solder the top and bottom corners. Unless you have an assistant available, use strips of masking tape to hold the pieces together while you solder. Do the same with the remaining sides, being sure to retain a 90° angle at each corner. Next, run solder down the inside and the outside of each corner joint.

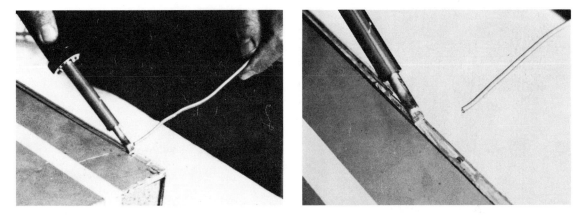

Spread solder along each edge of the terrarium, allowing the solder to flow completely over the entire foil surface.

Use the box itself as an outline for drawing a pattern for the bottom piece. This ensures an accurate fit. Double-strength window glass is best for the bottom piece (it will not show after you put plants in the finished terrarium). After cutting the bottom piece to pattern, attach copper foil as above and cover it with solder. Join the bottom piece to the sides and run solder into every joint

Solder the inside edges of the terrarium, allowing extra solder to fill in any open crevices.

After the sides and ends have been soldered together, place the box on a piece of paper and trace an exact outline to serve as a guide for cutting the bottom piece. After cutting the bottom piece, wrap the edges with foil and cover this with solder. Finally, attach the bottom piece, soldering all edges both inside and out.

inside and outside. Be sure to fill every crack and crevice with solder so that the seams will be watertight.

You can leave the silver color of the solder as it is on the finished piece or you can apply a patina to create a soft, antique effect. The two patinas available for antiquing produce a grey, lead-like appearance or a warm bronze finish. Brush the liquid patina on with a sable brush, or wipe it on with a rag. Allow it to sit for a few minutes, then rub over the soldered areas with a rag.

Wipe grey patina on soldered edges to produce an antique lead appearance.

Multifaceted Terrarium with Hinged Lid

The first step in planning this multifaceted terrarium is to draw a full-size pattern for the bottom piece. Then decide how far you want the terrarium to bow out around the middle. You can make a full-size pattern of this cross-section simply by drawing parallel lines at a fixed distance away from the edges of your first pattern. Finally, decide how high you want the finished terrarium to stand and you can work out a full-size pattern for the individual faces. Each of these is cut from the same pattern.

Choose your glass, a light color for the top to show off the plants and allow them enough light, a darker color or shade for the lower half. Cut the bottom piece and the lower faces, then the upper faces. Wait to cut the top until the rest of the terrarium is assembled.

Wrap the bottom and all of the faces with copper foil. Coat them with solder, then start attaching faces one at a time to the bottom piece. Tack them first with just a spot of solder as you may have to do some adjusting by the time you come to the last face. When all of the faces are in place, solder the joints solidly together and fill in any gaps with molten solder. Be especially sure to

Inventive designs such as this multifaced terrarium are easily carried out using the copper-foil method.

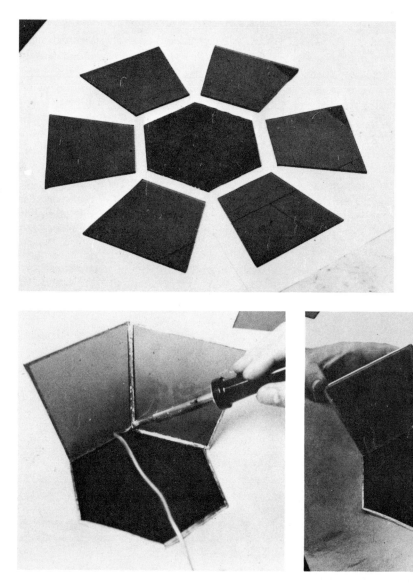

After cleaning the edges of the cut pieces with steel wool, wrap them with copper foil, and solder.

Spot-solder the angled sides to the base piece.

Spread solder evenly along all joints. Bring the solder and the tip of the iron together on the surface to be soldered. The heat from the iron will cause the solder to spread evenly.

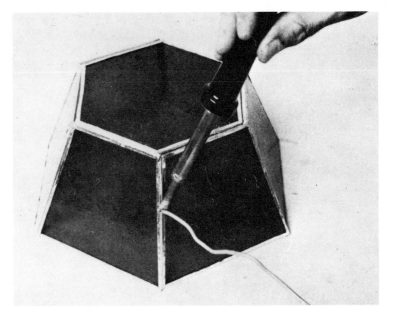

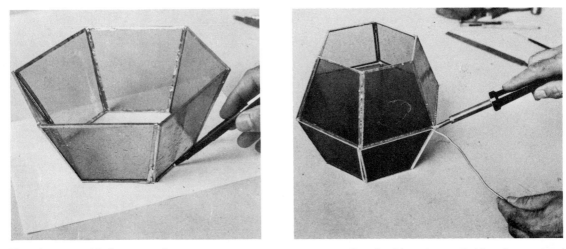

Use the assembled top section to trace an accurate pattern for the hinged top. Solder the top and bottom halves together.

solder the inside of all the joints at this stage of construction while you still have easy access. Fasten the top faces together also, using your full-size pattern to get the angles right.

Now make a pattern for the lid by drawing round the outside edge of the top section. This will ensure a perfect fit. Fasten the two halves together and solder along the entire length of all of

This simple handmade hinge is formed by shaping two interlocking U-shaped pieces and soldering one to the lid and the other to the side of the top section.

Use bronzing patina to harmonize copper edges with amber glass.

the joints. The soldering should make your terrarium water-tight. In case you do find a few open spaces later, you can fill them in with putty or something similar.

Make two small wire loops and attach them at the top corners of one of the upper faces. These eyes will serve to hold the lid in place. Use pliers to hold them while you solder them in position. This may seem like a job that requires three hands, but apply a small mound of solder first and then you can press the eye into place with your pliers in one hand while you melt the solder with the iron in your other hand.

Wrap the lid and coat it with solder. Use some more short lengths of wire to make the other part of the two hinges. These should lie right in place while you solder them firmly to the lid. Test your hinge and adjust it if necessary by bending the wires or attaching them differently.

Depending upon the color of glass you have chosen and whether you prefer a weathered look to that of shiny metal, you may want to cover the solder with a patina. If so, brush it on and rub it over the metal with a cloth. Amber glass harmonizes nicely with a bronze patina on the copper.

Stained Glass Hanging Ornament

Materials Checklist:
  Small pieces of stained glass
  Glass cutter
  Mat knife
  Needle-nosed pliers
  Soldering iron
  Solder with flux core
  $\frac{1}{8}''$ U-shaped lead came
  Steel wool

Imaginatively designed birds, insects, or other flying creatures are especially appropriate for a stained glass hanging ornament. Choose a subject that appeals to you and draw a full-size pattern simplifying the form into basic shapes that you can cut easily in glass. After you have sketched the design lightly with pencil or charcoal, strengthen the outlines with a black soft-tip marker. The outlines of the design must be heavy enough to show through the colored glass so that you can cut it directly over the pattern. To select the colors for the ornament, hold various pieces up to the light until you find a satisfying combination.

Kinds of Lead Came

This project introduces the use of lead, which craftsmen call *came*. The lead has channels in it to hold the pices of glass in position. Because lead is opaque in contrast to the transparency of glass, it appears as a black line against light. As a design element, it can function in a strong geometric way.

You can make all sorts of decorative designs into patterns for hanging ornaments or free-standing forms mounted on a solid base.

In planning any large project with lead, you must consider the dark area of the lead as well as the colors of the glass. For the butterfly ornament you will need only U-shaped came to outline the individual shapes, but most other types of came are used between two pieces of glass. Here are the standard shapes:

U-shaped came is used for edging panels and for lamp shade edges.

Standard H-shaped lead came ranges from $\frac{1}{4}$ inch to $1\frac{1}{2}$ inch in width. Half-round top came is used for decorative effect.

Came with an off-center heart is used for outer edges to allow more trimming area in window installations. Came with an open heart is used for insertion of reinforcing rods when it is desirable to hide them.

Right-angle came makes it easy to build three-dimensional objects.

Stained Glass Butterfly

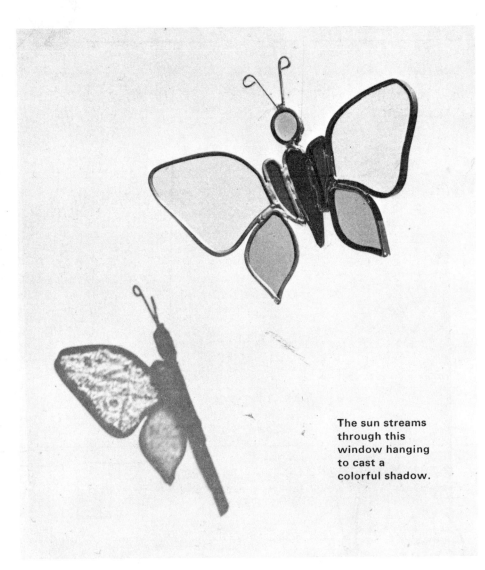

The sun streams
through this
window hanging
to cast a
colorful shadow.

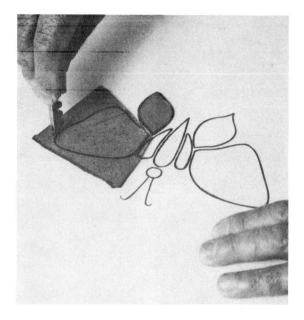

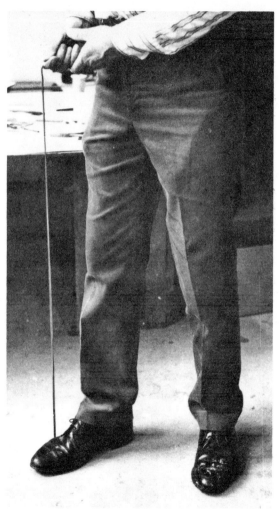

Cut the individual shapes, and wrap U-shaped came tightly round each piece. Before using the came, though, stretch it to straighten it and to take up any slack. Fasten one end in a vice and pull on the other end with pliers. For shorter pieces, catch one end under your foot and pull upwards.

Use a lead-cutting knife to cut the came so that the two ends butt together forming a joint or seam. Whenever possible, locate the seam where it will meet the seam of the adjacent piece when they are fastened together. You can make your own came knife by sharpening the reverse (bottom) side of an inexpensive linoleum-cutting knife. Use a firm, slightly rocking motion to cut through the lead. Keep your knife sharp.

Straighten the U-shaped came by stretching it as shown above.

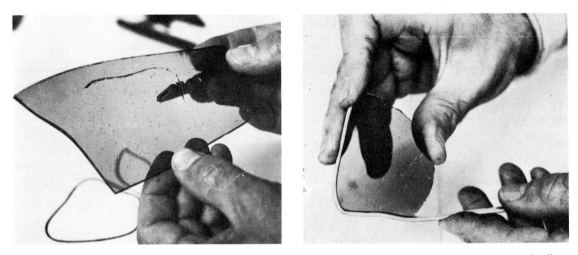

After you have scored irregularly shaped patterns, tap from below until a crack appears under the line. Wrap each individual piece of glass snugly with came.

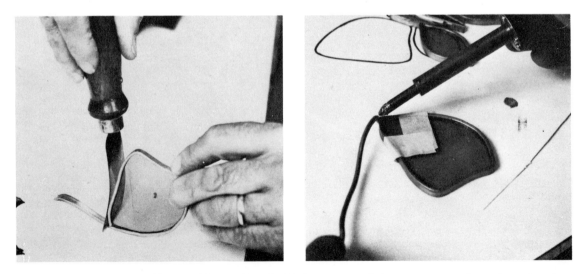

Trim neatly at the joint. Use masking tape to hold the corner of the came securely against the glass while soldering the joint.

30

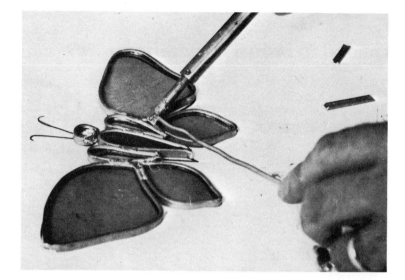

Solder the seam of each piece. If lead has been stored awhile, it may have an oxide formed on it which resists solder. Use fine steel wool to clean the came if necessary. Arrange the wrapped pieces in the form of the final ornament. Apply flux where the seam of one piece touches the seam of the adjacent piece. Solder the points together on the front side, then turn the ornament over and solder the same points on the back.

File off any unattractive lumps of solder. Bend the wings carefully so that the ornament takes on a three-dimensional form. Solder a wire loop on top at the balancing point. Use clear nylon fishing line to hang the ornament in a window where it can catch and reflect sunlight.

When the solder is cool, bend the ornament into a three-dimensional shape.

31

Leaded Window Medallion

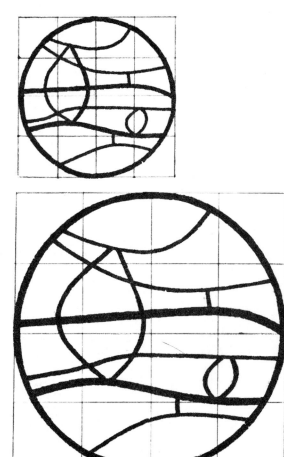

Additional Materials Checklist:
  $\frac{3}{16}''$ or $\frac{1}{4}''$ H-shaped lead came
  Metal vice
  Lead-cutting knife (a linoleum knife sharpened
    on the outside curve)
  $1''$ nails
  Small hammer
  White lead putty
  Putty knife
  Commercial whiting
  Scrub brushes
  Steel wool

Any window in your home can be made lovely and inviting by the introduction of a leaded glass medallion, attractive on the inside by day and colorful on the outside by night. The technique of producing leaded glass windows has varied little since medieval craftsmen created the inspired windows of the great cathedrals. We now use extruded lead cames (grooved rods) instead of casting them ourselves, an electric soldering iron rather than one heated in a fire and a steel-wheeled glass cutter instead of a hot rod of iron—other than this, the essentials of the craft remain the same.

In planning a project of this magnitude, you will want to follow the professional practice of making several preliminary designs to scale—$1''$ or $\frac{1}{2}''$ to $1'$ is customary. Stained glass designers use

You can enlarge a small-scale drawing to actual size by "squaring off" and transferring it free-hand to a set of larger squares.

pen and India or Pelican ink to indicate lead lines and watercolor paints to fill in the colored glass areas as this closely approximates the final effect of the panel. First measure the pane of glass in the window that the medallion will be placed in and then, using a pencil, sketch in your design lightly to the above scale. Block in the lead lines and border with India ink and apply transparent washes of watercolor (India ink is not dissolved by watercolor). Several sketches can be made to try different effects—colors, lead widths, etc. The basic shape of the medallion can be rectangular, diamond-shaped or circular. Fruit or vegetable forms in a circular shape can be simply designed for easy leading.

The Cartoon

When you have decided on the final design, you must then enlarge the small sketch to full size (this is called a "cartoon"—the artist's traditional name for full-size detailed drawings). If your design is simple, you may be able to draw it freehand in full size following your small sketch. Most artists, however, enlarge by "squaring off." This is accomplished by dividing your sketch into squares and dividing your full-size paper into an equal number of squares. You then transfer the design from each small square to the larger square. The full-size drawing must be done with great accuracy as all dimensions of the actual glass panel are taken from it. Color selection, however, is usually made from the original color sketch.

Charcoal is an excellent medium for this full-size drawing. Lines can be easily changed and shifted when necessary, yet it is black enough

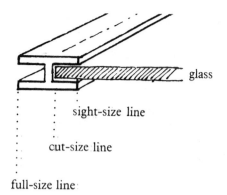

glass

sight-size line

cut-size line

full-size line

for indication of lead lines. When you are satisfied with the look of it, spray it with fixative to prevent smudging.

Three vital measurements are indicated on the drawing above:

1. Full-size line—this represents the outer edge or perimeter of the finished panel.

2. Sight-size line—this indicates the inside line of the lead came.

3. Cut-size line—this shows where the glass itself will end when inserted into the came.

Once your full-size cartoon is complete, you still need two additional full-size sheets—one for paper patterns for cutting glass, and one as a working drawing to serve as a leading guide.

Put two blank sheets on a table with the full-size cartoon on the top and pieces of carbon paper in between. Tack through the corners of all three sheets and carbons so that the papers will not shift as you trace the lines. While the sheets are still tacked down, number each individual segment that will be a cut piece of glass. Start numbering at the lower left and end with the upper right segments. Later on, when the pattern is cut apart,

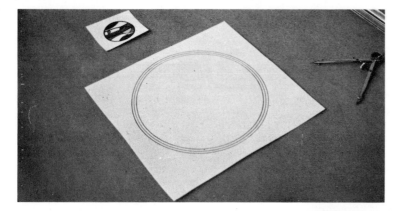

You must clearly mark the full-size, sight-size and cut-size lines of the outside lead came on the cartoon before indicating the inside lead lines.

you will keep the numbered paper pattern with the piece of cut glass so you will always know its relative position in the panel. Also write the appropriate color name on each pattern.

Separate the sheets and you are ready to cut your paper patterns from one of the copies. A professional double-bladed pattern shears is useful here but not really essential. Two single-edge razor blades taped together with a $\frac{1}{16}''$ wood or cardboard spacer in between make a good substitute (see drawing).

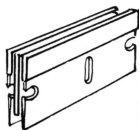

You can put together a homemade pattern cutter with two razor blades and a spacer.

Mark each of the three sheets for later identification by labelling the top paper "cartoon," the middle "paper pattern" and the bottom "working drawing."

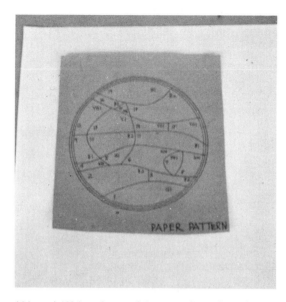

PAPER PATTERN

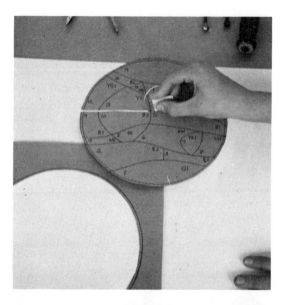

(Above) Write the position number of each segment at the left side of each paper pattern, the color name or number at the right side. (Right) First cut the long major lines which divide the panel, then the smaller subdivisions.

The two razor blades or shears cut the paper pattern to the cut-size for each piece of glass, allowing for the width of the lead heart which comes between the pieces of glass. Cut the outer perimeter cut-size line with a single blade. As you cut out the paper patterns, place them in their correct position on top of the second copy, your working drawing.

Keep the paper patterns in order as you cut them so that you will be able to place them back on the cartoon easily.

Arrange the paper patterns for the same color to take maximum advantage of the glass piece.
←

Score the more difficult curves first, then the other cuts.

←

Before starting to lead, check the fit of the cut segments by arranging them in position on top of the full-size cartoon.

Now cut the pieces of selected glass using the paper pattern as shown in the illustration. Glass must be cut very accurately to the paper pattern or leading will be difficult. As each pattern of glass is cut, return it to its proper place on the working drawing (with its paper pattern). When all pieces are cut, you are ready to begin leading. Take the glass segments off your working drawing and arrange them in numerical sequence next to your work bench or table. Staple or tape your working drawing to the top of your work bench.

When stretching short pieces of lead came, pull with just enough force to straighten the lead.

Run a sharpened pencil dipped in linseed oil down each groove to open the flanges of the lead came. Opening them allows different thicknesses of stained glass to fit into the came.

Before lead came is used, it must be stretched to straighten it and to take up any slack. A vice and pliers are the only tools you need. Tighten one end of the lead in a vice. Grip the other end firmly with the pliers and pull with enough pressure so that a 6′ length of lead stretches 2″ or 3″. Leads must also be opened up by running a sharpened pencil through each groove to force the edges apart.

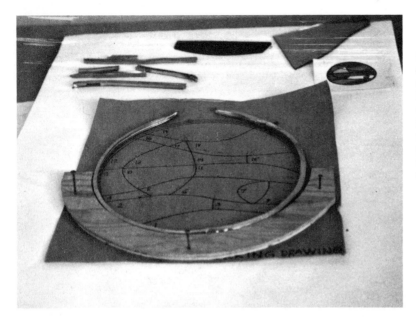

Run the perimeter came around the form, pressing it up against the wood. Use U-shaped came for the outside border if the medallion is to be free hanging. Use off-center H-shaped came which provides extra trimming space to install windows in specific openings.

Make a cut-out in a piece of $\frac{1}{4}''$ plywood that is the exact size and shape of the opening in which the window will be placed. If you are making a free-hanging medallion, cut the form to its finished size and shape. Nail the plywood over the working drawing. You may find it easier to cut the form in half, nailing the top part in place only after you have finished leading the bottom section of the medallion. Butt a piece of $\frac{1}{4}''$ came up against the plywood, running it completely around the perimeter. Allow the ends to overlap an inch or two when you cut it. A handy, inexpensive tool for cutting lead can be made by sharpening the reverse (bottom) side of a linoleum cutting knife. A firm, slightly rocking motion directly down on the lead is the best way to cut.

Now insert the first piece of glass into the lead grooves at the lower left. Tap the glass in slightly with the wooden handle of your knife. Now place a piece of lead along the top of the glass, fitting the glass into the groove. Add the second piece of glass and lead and continue following the numbered sequence. Where leads meet at the joints, fit the end of one into the side of the other or butt them. Put all the pieces of glass and lead down in this manner until the medallion is complete. Then bring together the open, perimeter came ends, and cut and solder where they join. Carefully tap the lead came flat at each joint with a hammer.

Soldering each of the joints comes next. Set your soldering iron to heat and, when it is hot,

Slip the point of the lead cutting knife under the ends of the lead strips and bend them up slightly so that the next piece of lead will fit into them easily. ⟶

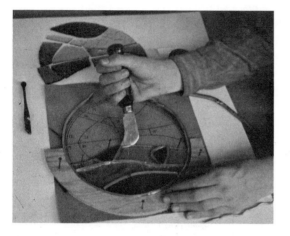

Trim off the ends of the lead strips as close to the glass as possible without actually touching the glass itself.

Be sure that the iron tip is touching and heating the lead as you feed solder into the joint.

touch solder and the iron tip to the joint simultaneously. The solder should flow evenly over the joint, although to do this may take a little practice. Fortunately, joints that are not soldered too smoothly have that interesting "handmade" look.

39

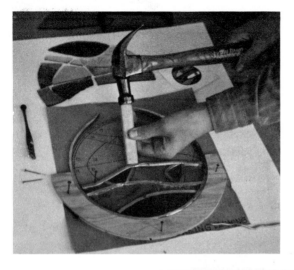

When all of the joints on one side are soldered, remove the plywood form and carefully hold the panel up to the light. At this point you can, if necessary, change a color or replace a cracked piece of glass. Put the panel down with the unsoldered side up. Pry up the lead rim around the piece to be changed. Cut a fresh piece of glass slightly smaller than the first one and put it in place. Press the lead down again and solder at the joints around this piece. When you are satisfied with the appearance of the panel, solder up all the joints on this side.

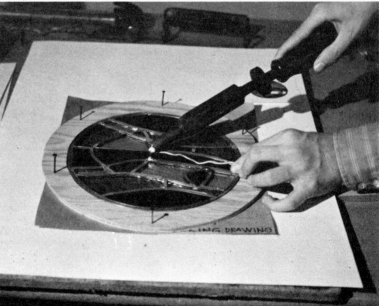

Turn the panel over and fit it once again into the form before soldering the back joints.

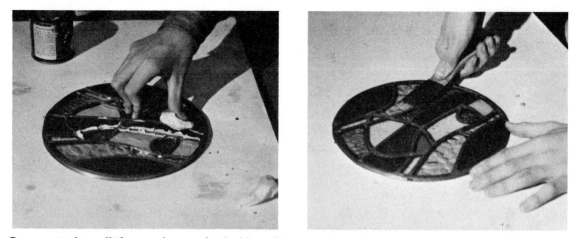

Press putty into all the openings on both sides of the panel in order to weatherproof it completely. Use a stiff-bladed putty knife to press down the face of the lead strips.

The final process before installing your medallion is to putty the panel. Lay the panel flat on your work table and, with your thumb and fingers, press white lead putty into all the lead grooves on one side of the panel to seal them. Carefully press down on all the leads with a putty knife and cut off any excess putty with a sharp piece of wood. Repeat this operation on the other side of the panel to make it fully weatherproof. Sprinkle whiting on the panel and scrub with a stiff brush to clean off any remaining putty or dirt. Finally, polish with a soft cloth.

To make a form for large rectangular panels, simply nail $\frac{1}{4}''$-thick wooden strips to a plywood base along the full-size lines. Panels that exceed about $12'' \times 24''$ need reinforcing bars across the back for support. Put $\frac{3}{8}''$ wide galvanized iron bars at right angles to the panel and solder them to both edges and to each lead they cross.

To give the lead a silvery shine, polish it with fine steel wool and then coat it with clear lacquer.

Stained Glass Lighting Fixture

Additional Materials Checklist:
  Light socket, cord, and supporting chain

This project demonstrates how stained glass can be used to create attractive three-dimensional objects. A hanging lamp of stained glass fills an area with both color and light. Using the same techniques, a lamp shade, a lantern, even an unusual waste basket can be easily made.

Your design sketch in this case should be in perspective, for you to properly visualize the final effect. The basic form of the fixture illustrated is octagonal and it is best to use a dense, translucent glass which will diffuse the light of the electric bulb.

Before you start construction, use color sketches to determine which colors and shades of glass to use in order to create the effect you want. First assemble and solder the main section of the lamp flat. Then bend the soft lead into the finished shape. As you add each piece of glass, tap it into the lead grooves.

Use nails as you proceed with the leading to keep the glass and came securely in place. Since the short horizontal leads are the same length, you can cut them all beforehand to save trimming time.

The main wrap-around section of the fixture is fabricated first following the same procedure as for a flat leaded panel. Use $\frac{1}{4}''$ U-shaped lead came for all edge leading and $\frac{1}{8}''$-wide H-shaped came for the other leads.

When the main section is completely leaded and soldered, carefully stand it upright and bend the panel a little bit at a time at each vertical lead until the two edges meet, forming the octagon. Solder the joint where the two edges meet.

Using the completed main section as a guide, draw a full-size pattern for the top section. Lead this section in the same way as the main section, leaving an opening at the top for the cord to the light socket to pass through.

Use a minimum amount of solder on the joints so that the vertical leads will bend easily.

Bend the lamp body equally at each vertical lead, bringing the ends slowly together.

To hold the ends together for proper soldering, put a piece of string or a strong rubber band around the lamp body.

(Right) A light socket, cord, supporting chain, and accessories are all the additional materials you'll need to complete your lighting fixture.

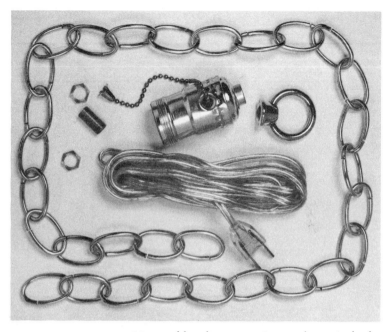

(Below) Pass a curved piece of lead through the bottom link of the hanging chain and then solder it to the top of the fixture.

Now solder the top section to the main body. To finish off the edge where the two sections meet, a piece of $\frac{1}{4}''$ flat lead (which you can cut from the $\frac{1}{4}''$ came) can be soldered all round, covering any unevenness in the joints.

Finally, insert a standard light socket with cord into the lantern, allowing the cord to pass through the opening at the top. Secure the socket with solder. Attach a supporting chain to the top of the lantern by running a piece of flat lead through the bottom link of the chain and soldering the ends to the top section.

Stained Glass Candlestick Holder

Pleasant changes in aspect from daytime to night are inherent in projects such as candlesticks. By day the light filters through the glass, constantly changing in angle and intensity. At night, with the candles lit, the holder provides its own illumination, casting flickering patterns of color on surrounding areas.

Traditional lead came is H-shaped, with a channel on each side for glass. It is used to fill in between two pieces of glass in a flat plane. A

Cut angled pieces accurately to pattern.

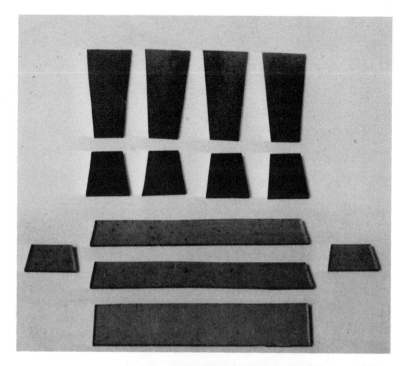

Open the groove of the lead came with the round end of the glass cutter.

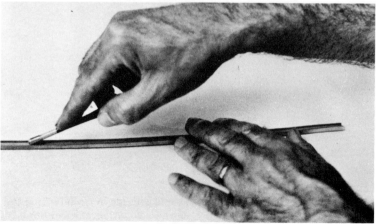

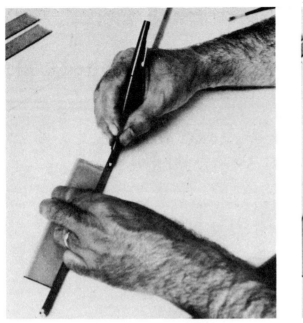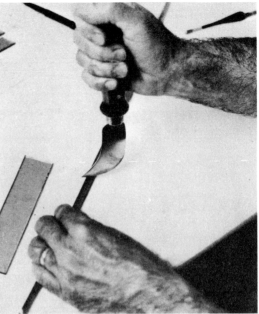

Draw the mitred corner on the right-angled came and cut with a sharp lead-cutting knife.

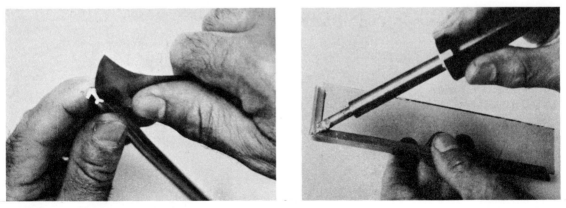

Open the end of the lead came where it is pressed in from cutting the mitred corner. Solder the mitred corners together one at a time.

Attractive stained-glass hanging ornaments reflect constantly changing patterns of color and light. These pieces of glass are enclosed in strips of U-shaped lead came which is available in a variety of widths. The lead is seen as a dark opaque line against the light, setting off the beauty of the glass colors.

A

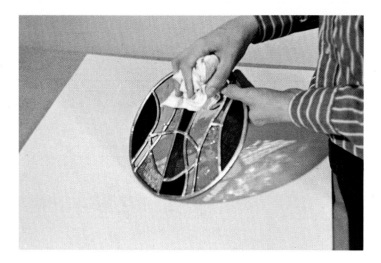

To give the lead a silvery shine, polish it with fine steel wool and then coat it with clear lacquer.

The shimmer and texture of stained glass is accentuated by the light and shade of the outside view.

B

A large, neat table top is essential when you are working with the many small pieces of glass that go into a stained-glass lamp shade. A piece of old carpet tacked on the bench top provides an excellent surface for cutting glass.

The completed lamp shade or hanging lighting fixture is an attractive three-dimensional object that fills an area with both color and light.

C

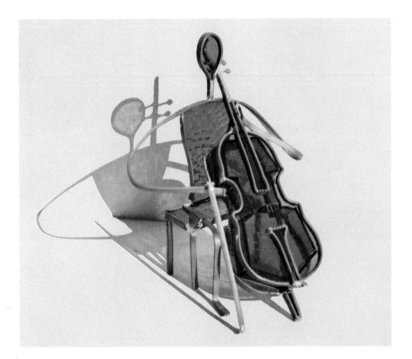

Lead came is a strong, yet flexible, metal strip which binds glass together in three-dimensional forms of all kinds.

The reflections cast by textured stained glass are often as fascinating as the work itself.

D

New techniques using clear epoxy adhesives in combination with adhesive-backed copper foil open the way to much freer expression with stained glass.

Stained-glass candlesticks glow by day with reflected natural illumination and, at night, with their own flickering candlelight.

The natural beauty of plant forms is enhanced when you view them through the subtle colors and textures of a stained-glass terrarium. This multifaceted example was constructed with the copper-foil technique. The antique-copper look was achieved by brushing a liquid patina over the soldered surfaces.

F

A box terrarium constructed with the copper-foil technique is strong enough to hold the weight of earth, plants and small rocks.

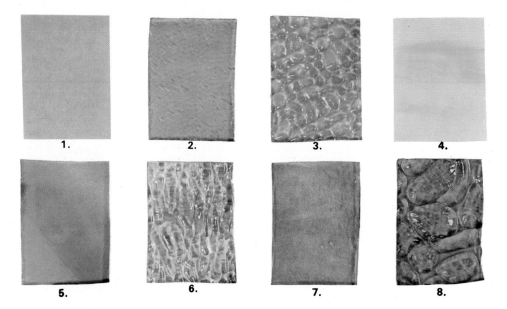

1.   **2.**   **3.**   **4.**

5.   **6.**   **7.**   **8.**

Stained glass is available in a wide variety of colors and textures, suitable for many kinds of imaginative projects. Some common types of glass shown here are: (1.) Handblown antique; (2.) Seedy antique; (3.) Granite-textured cathedral; (4.) Opalescent; (5.) English streaky; (6.) Variegated cathedral; (7.) American Blenko; (8.) Pebble-textured cathedral.

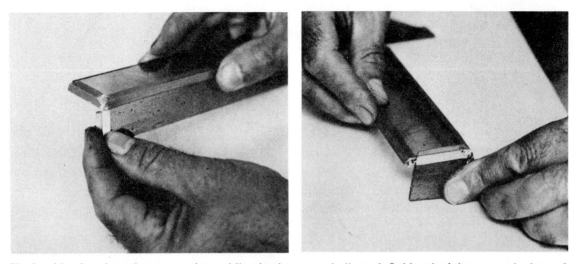

Fit the side piece into the top section, adding lead came as indicated. Solder the joints as each piece of came is added. Hold glass in place to measure the next piece of lead.

recent development is right-angle lead which affords the artist an alternative to the copper-foil method for creating three-dimensional objects.

An accurate perspective drawing will serve you both as a guide and an indication of how the completed project will appear. After choosing the glass and cutting all the pieces to pattern, you can start construction using the angled lead came. The channels in the lead must be opened slightly with a round piece of wood or an old lead pencil. Open them just enough to accommodate the thicknesses of the glass you are working with.

For a smooth finish, mitre the joints when you work with angled lead. Cut the lead carefully with a very sharp lead-cutting knife. Start with the base of the candlestick holder, cutting the long pieces first, then the shorter side pieces. Test the pieces of lead by taping them to the glass. Make

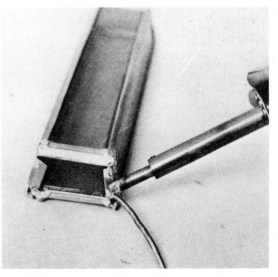

Fill in any open joints with extra solder.

49

Tape the upper section of the holder together while soldering U-shaped lead to the top edges. Use a small amount of solder on the top edge joints so that they may be smoothed off with very little filing.

Smooth off uneven joints with a steel file.

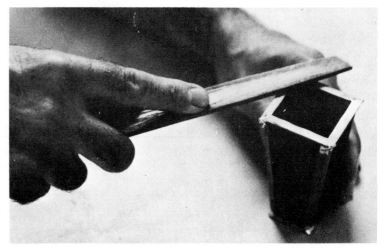

any trimming adjustments necessary. Solder the joints when the fit is perfect.

Now construct the top units of the holder, the chimneys that will surround the candles. This time use angle lead for the vertical side pieces, U-shaped lead for the top and bottom of each section.

Before soldering the top units to the base, file down all the joints and edges with a steel file. Use steel wool for a final cleaning and polishing, then solder the top units to the base. To retain the silvery appearance of the polished lead, brush on clear lacquer.

Polish with steel wool prior to coating with clear lacquer. Solder the top units to the base to complete assembly.

Leaded Glass Figurines

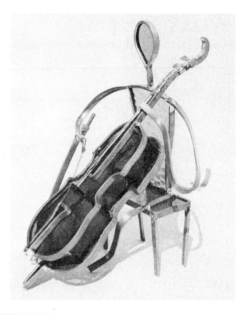

A scale-model musical instrument complete with musician made entirely from lead and stained glass is a unique home decoration for a shelf or coffee table.

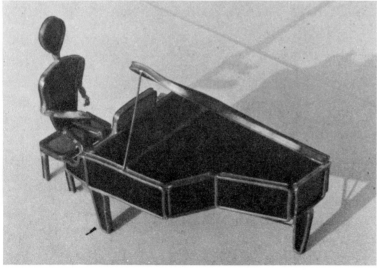

Three-dimensional stained-glass objects not only reflect color and light from their many different angles but also cast interesting shadow patterns.

Stained Glass Piano and Pianist

Musical instruments built to scale and fabricated with stained glass make a charming home ornament. A piano with a seated pianist is a relatively easy project. Since the measurements for this project must be exact, you need to make a preliminary mock-up from heavy paper or light cardboard.

Look at an actual piano or a photograph and make a sketch simplifying each part into a flat plane. Now cut and fit paper patterns for each element in the piano. Fasten the paper patterns together with tape. Adjust or remake any parts necessary to produce a perfectly fitted, correctly proportioned model. Do the same with the figure and stool. Number each paper pattern and mark it with the color of glass to be used. The piece of striped opalescent glass will make an ideal keyboard.

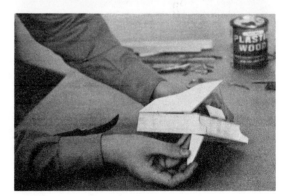

Remove the tape and accurately cut the glass pieces according to the patterns. Wrap the individual pieces in H-shaped came, soldering each joint. Next assemble the main body of the piano by soldering the top and bottom of each piece. Use tape or rubber bands to hold the model together while soldering. Use several thin pieces of wire as reinforcing rods to stabilize the legs and to support the open top. Clean and polish the model.

A piano, of course, is just one of many forms that can be reproduced in miniature. Animals, birds, boats, and antique cars are only a few of the other possibilities. Abstract, three-dimensional stained glass constructions are an exciting art form.

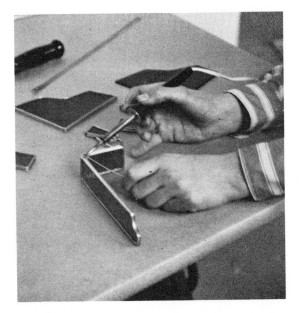

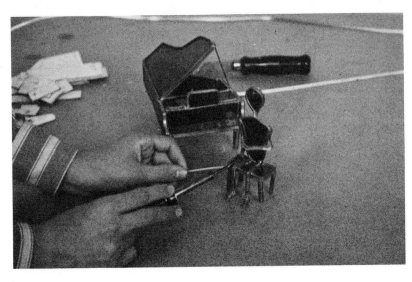

Use lead strips which can be bent easily into position for the arms and legs of the figure.

Stained Glass Cello and Cellist

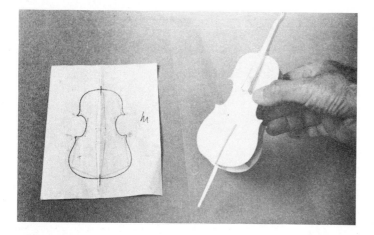

Work out a full-size model using stiff paper which will then be used as a pattern for cutting the glass.

Try to look at an actual instrument or at least a good photograph of one while you make a scale sketch. Simplify the forms as much as possible into flat planes so that you will be able to cut them out of glass sheet. Curved parts have to be simulated with several small flat pieces placed together. Using the scale sketch as a guide, cut and fit cardboard patterns for each part of the cello and cellist. Tape the parts together with masking tape, adjusting and trimming each part until it fits perfectly. Remake any parts necessary to produce a perfectly fitted, correctly proportioned model. Number each pattern, at the same time indicating the color of glass. Use middle-to-light value glass, since after assembly you will be looking through more than one layer of glass.

Follow the dotted lines for the initial cuts of the cello face piece.

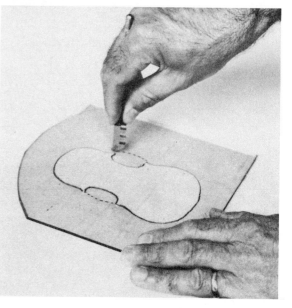

Remove the tape and use the individual patterns to cut the glass accurately. Wrap the top and bottom pieces of the cello with U-shaped lead came. Use masking tape to hold the lead in place and solder all of the seams. The side pieces of the cello are so small that it is best to glue them to the top and to the bottom with clear epoxy glue. Quick-drying (about 4 minutes) clear epoxy is readily available and holds the pieces together with great strength. Add the fingerboard, which you can shape out of a piece of came, the pegs, and the supporting rod at the bottom of the cello. Simulate the strings with fine copper wire, using epoxy to fasten them to the little stained glass bridge which you also glue to the top of the cello.

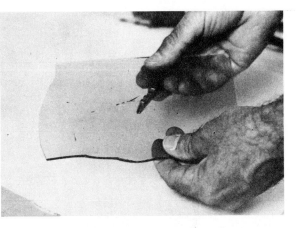

Tap gently all along initial score line.

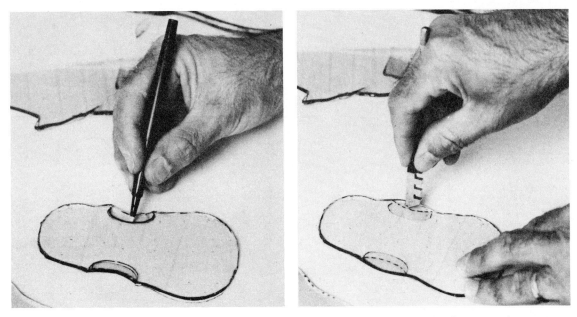

Mark in the curves with a soft-tip marker. Follow the dotted lines for the first curved cuts.

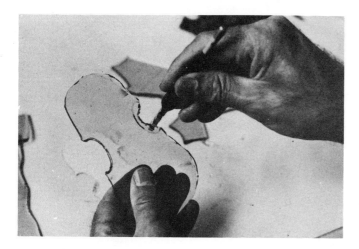

Carefully and slowly groze out the glass until the final curve is achieved.

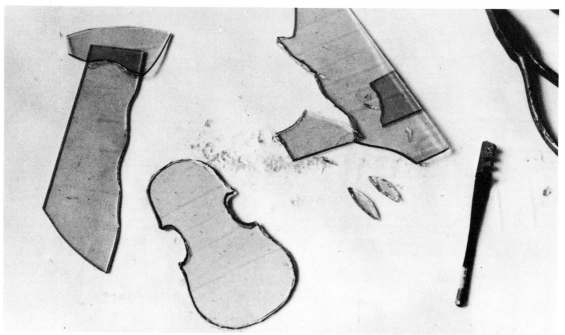

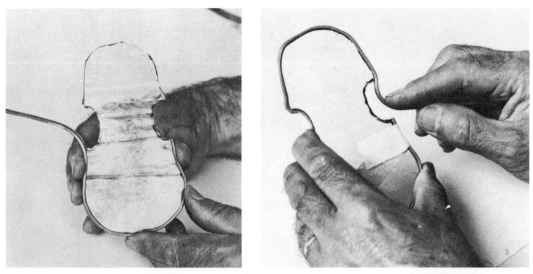

Wrap U-shaped came around the cello face piece. Press came firmly into the deep curves.

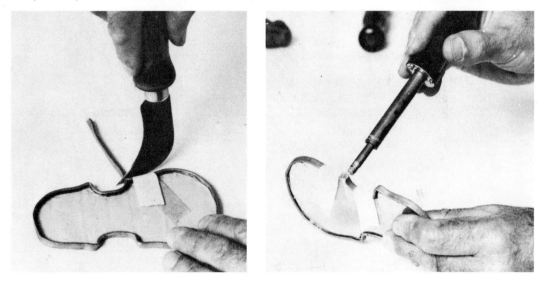

Trim the came neatly and solder at the joint.

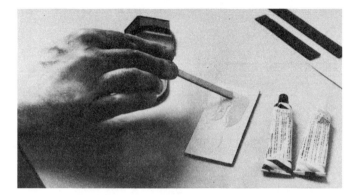

Mix the two epoxy components together with a stick and a scrap piece of cardboard.

Dip the edge of the small glass piece into the freshly mixed epoxy.

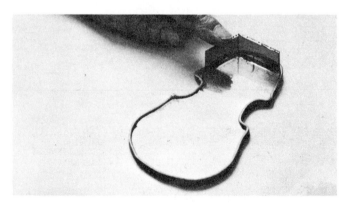

Hold glued sections in place until the epoxy hardens.

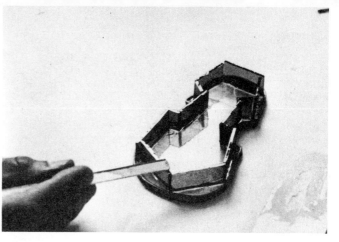

When the sections are all glued on one side spread fresh epoxy on the top surfaces.

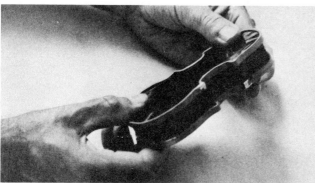

To complete assembly of the cello body add the back piece, holding the unit together by hand until the epoxy hardens.

Bend lead into fingerboard shape using grozing pliers. Join the fingerboards and the base piece to the cello body with solder.

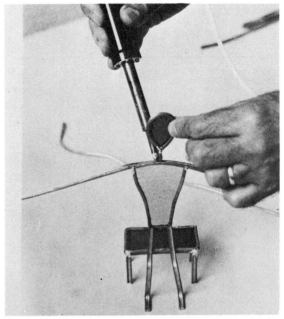

(Top) Cut glass pieces for the cellist directly over a paper pattern. Solder all joints to assemble the cellist and stool.

(Left) Allow extra width in the lead arm pieces for twisting arms into position.

62

Assemble and solder the cellist in a similar manner. When both cello and cellist are complete, arrange them together. Since the lead remains flexible, you can change the position from time to time.

Bend the ends of the arms into hand positions. Arms can be repositioned for either resting or for playing the cello.

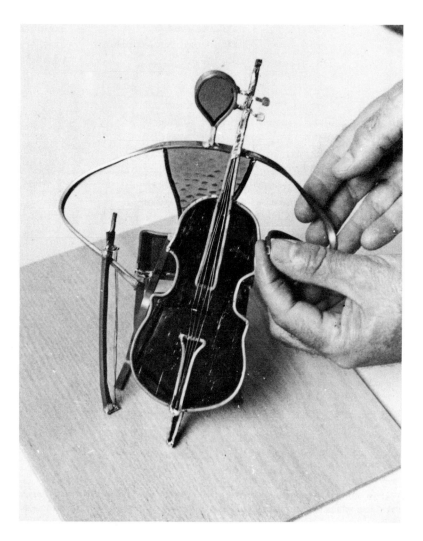

Stained Glass Lamp Shade

Additional Materials Checklist:

Opalescent glass	Toothpicks
Plastic foam (Styrofoam) form	Tracing paper
Gesso	Lamp parts and wiring

A moderate amount of experience in working with glass and ordinary equipment is all that is needed to create beautiful lamp shades in either Tiffany or contemporary style. Plastic foam lamp shade forms in a variety of sizes and shapes are available ready-made from stained glass suppliers, but the creative craftsman can make his own from plastic foam or soft wood.

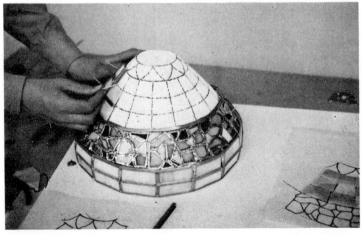

A large, neat table top is essential when you are working with the many small pieces of glass that go into a stained-glass lamp shade. A piece of old carpet tacked on the bench top provides an excellent surface for cutting glass.

To make your own shade form, glue layers of plastic foam (Styrofoam) together and place a weight on top of them while they dry overnight.

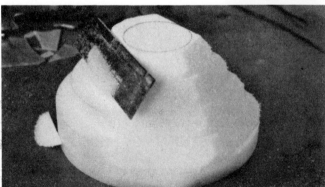

Use a coping saw, a backsaw as shown here, or a hack saw blade to shape the plastic foam form.

A relatively simple shape is the best choice for your first lamp shade project. A curved form about 12″ across at the bottom and 3″ at the top is easily worked. Draw a full-size profile of the basic form on heavy paper. If a block of plastic foam thick enough for the entire form is not available, glue three or four layers together with white glue or rubber cement until the correct height of 8″ is achieved. Using the paper profile as a guide, cut the plastic foam to shape with a coping saw. Final adjustment to the exact shape is accomplished with a block of wood covered with rough sandpaper. Give the surface a final smoothing with fine sandpaper.

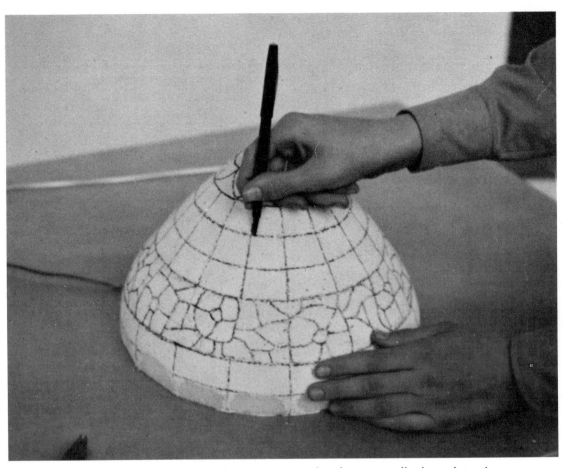

Draw in the lines of the design so they are dark enough to be seen easily through tracing paper.

Paint the outer surface of the form with two coats of white gesso. When this is dry, use charcoal to draw the lampshade design directly onto the surface of the form. The charcoal lines are easily wiped off, allowing for changes. Use a felt-tip marker to establish the final lead lines of the design. The general color scheme can be indicated by coloring between the lines with colored felt-tip markers, giving a good idea of what the completed lamp shade will look like.

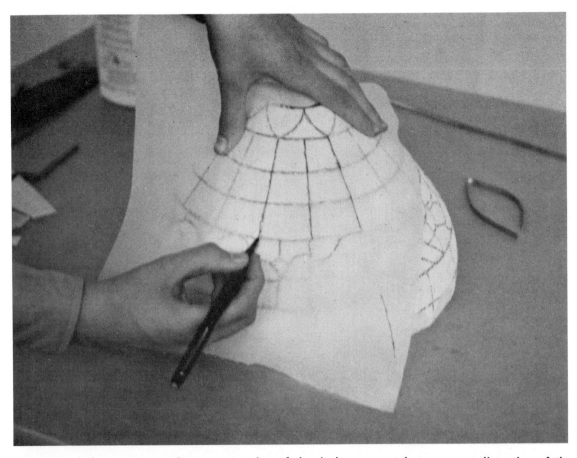

On a curved shape, trace each quarter section of the design separately to prevent distortion of the drawing.

Once the design is finalized on the plastic foam form, copy the patterns onto tracing paper, transferring this to a flat drawing which you will use as a cutting guide for the glass. Number each paper pattern and indicate your color selection.

Since the design on the form will serve as the leading guide, only the one flat drawing is needed. Use pattern shears or two razor blades taped together to cut out the paper patterns.

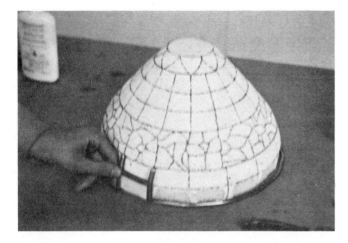

As the leading progresses, you can use toothpicks stuck into the plastic foam to hold the sections together and in place on the form.

Until you have some experience with soldering, you may find it easier to solder the joints each time you add a piece of glass and lead came to the shade.

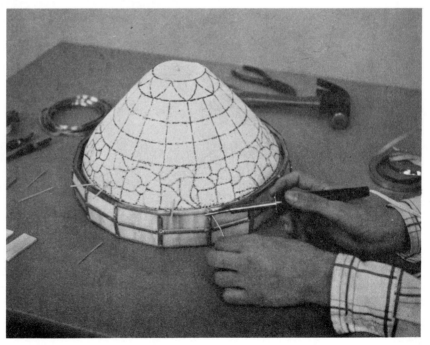

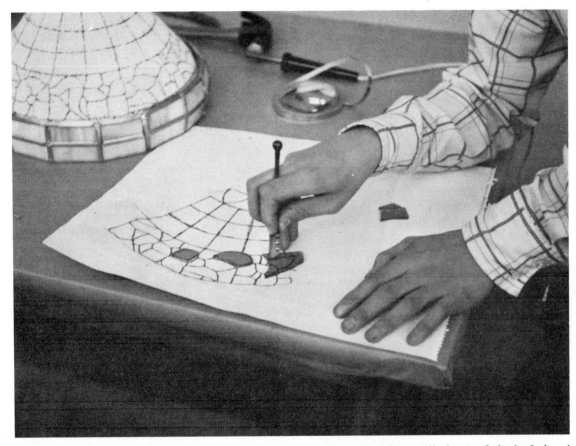

To simplify cutting and leading, use glass of uniform thickness for the small pieces of the leafy band. You can cut light-color glass directly over the pattern.

When all of the glass has been selected and cut to pattern, begin leading at the bottom of the form with a circle of U-shaped came (channel up). Butt and solder the joint of the first piece of came. Next place the first piece of glass in position. Use $\frac{3}{16}''$ H-shaped lead came as indicated by the design. Stick toothpicks into the form to hold both glass and lead in place. After leading the first row of glass pieces, solder each joint.

The backing of the copper foil is self-sticking and will hold tightly when pressed firmly around the edge of a piece of glass.

Continue leading upwards to where the leaf and flower shapes begin. For these you will use $\frac{1}{8}''$ H-shaped came instead of the $\frac{3}{16}''$-wide material as it will be easier to follow the more complex shapes with the thinner lead. Solder the joints as soon as you have leaded six or seven pieces.

The Copper Foil Method

Stained glass craftsmen use the so-called copper foil method to construct lamp shades when the design is unusually intricate. The preliminary steps up to the cutting of the paper patterns are the same. At this point, however, a single-edge razor or a mat knife must be used to cut the paper patterns since the foil does not take up any appreciable amount of space between the glass pieces.

When all the glass pieces have been cut to pattern, each edge is wrapped in adhesive-backed copper foil. The final assembly is done from the bottom of the shade upwards and each piece is held with toothpicks as with the leaded technique. Solder is applied along all of the seams and at every joint. The film of solder flows between the pieces of glass and over the surface of the copper foil. The appearance of the finished shade is the same as one made with traditional lead came.

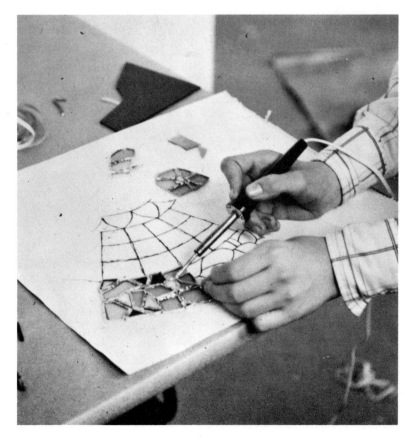

Spot solder each section of glass directly over the paper pattern spread out on a flat surface. Then place the section on the form and curve it gently into position.

Solder the sections of glass together on the form. If you use the copper foil method for the leafy band, solder the edges into the lead channel.

Lamp shades are normally made of opalescent glass which not only diffuses the light well, but is also opaque enough to hide the bulb and socket on the inside of the shade. Color selections for the shade depend upon individual taste, but analogous colors such as blue-green, blue, and blue-violet will give a harmonious glow to the shade while strong contrasting colors create a bright, lively effect. In the lampshade illustrated here, white milky glass was used for the main rectangular pieces to set off the band of brighter colors of the leaf and fruit shapes.

You can easily fill in any small openings between the pieces of glass in the leafy band with a drop or two of solder.

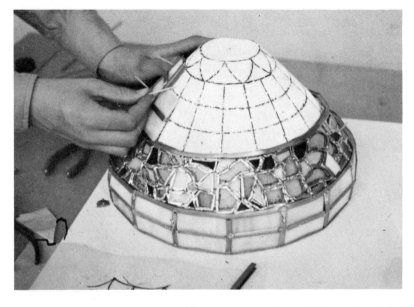

Where many lead strips are to be the same length, you may want to pre-cut them for faster assembly.

After all of the face joints are soldered, carefully re-move the shade from the form and solder the inside of all the joints. For greater stability, curve heavy wire around the inside and solder it in place.

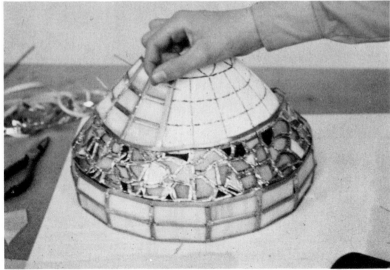

For final assembly, you need a bulb socket and fittings. These are of various types depending upon whether you are making a hanging lamp or attaching it to a base. Electrical supply shops or hardware dealers can supply the materials and show you how to connect them.

Finish off the top edge of the shade once again using U-shaped came. Finally, remove the shade from the form and solder all the joints on the inside. If necessary, heavy wire can be curved, fitted, and soldered to the inside perimeter of the shade. A hanging strap must be soldered across the top of the shade. Bore a hole in the center of the hanging strap for the lamp rod.

Some of the most popular Tiffany type shades are:

A few contemporary type shades are:

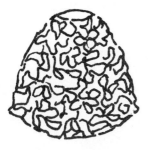

Stained Glass Bouquet with Vase

A stained glass bouquet of flowers and leaves not only makes a sparkling and unusual centrepiece for a dining or living room table, it also

presents an opportunity to experiment with some unorthodox techniques. This is a chance to combine and adapt some of the techniques of the previous projects. For example, use the copper-foil method for the leaves, the flowers which have simple petal shapes, and the vase. For more delicate flowers or where a lighter feeling seems called for, use quick-drying epoxy glue.

A few freehand sketches with a soft-tip marker will suggest possible designs, but don't feel bound by conventional floral shapes. Thin, delicate forms, fat chunky shapes, flowing curved pieces, can all be utilized. While you sketch out full-size floral shapes, remember that they will be grouped together as an arrangement. If you vary the size and shape of each flower it will give interest to the finished bouquet. Check your scrap box for bits of glass which may suggest leaf or petal shapes. When you have six or seven sketches completed, select stained glass colors for each sketch. Some flowers will look better with all of the petals the same color, while others will be more attactive with vari-colored petals.

Work first those designs for which copper foil seems most appropriate. Then turn to those designs which are best fabricated with epoxy glue. After selecting the colors for the different designs, cut glass to pattern over the designs.

Where you use the copper-foil method, you can achieve a three-dimensional form by tilting each petal as you solder it to the adjacent petal. For flowers with long slender petals, you can wrap the ends of the glass pieces with a little foil, cover the foil with solder, then join the petals together with additional solder. Let the petals spread out naturally at the other end.

Score petal shapes freely without being too bound by the drawn pattern.

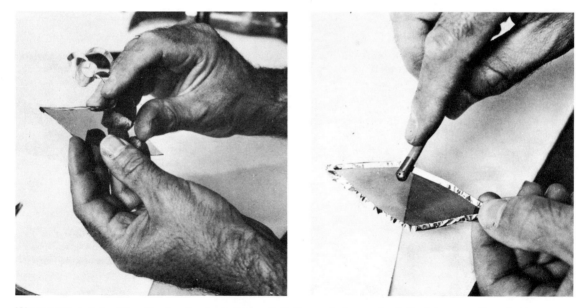

Wrap each petal with adhesive-backed copper foil. Smooth down the foil with a pencil or the handle of your glass cutter until it adheres tightly to the glass.

After cleaning the glass edges with steel wool, follow the basic copper-foil technique. First wrap the individual pieces with foil and stick it smoothly to the glass edge. Next, coat with oleic acid and cover all surfaces with solder.

Remember to solder the outside edge of the glass pieces as well as the inside edges.

Holding each petal at an angle, solder the ends together one at a time.

(Left) After making final adjustments to the petals, solder the leaf pieces to the main wire stem.

81

Some flowers look better with all of the petals the same color, while others are more attractive with varicolored petals.

Cover the ends of each piece of glass with copper foil, then coat with solder.

Solder the ends of the glass pieces together, forming a sunburst pattern.

Solder the stem to the middle of the glass cluster.

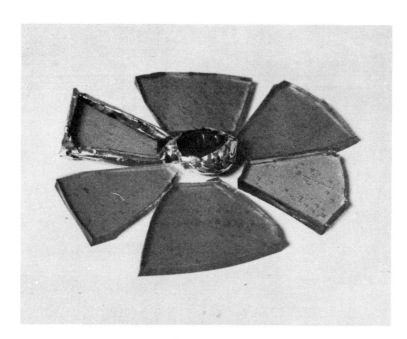

Glass beads available in a variety of colors and sizes add a jewel-like appearance to floral designs.

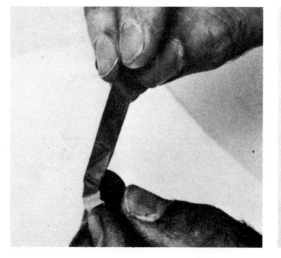

Use your creativity to combine glass beads with cut glass pieces in floral designs.

Flowers which are to be glued need to have waxed paper underneath them to keep them from sticking to your work surface. Use curved objects, such as an old soup bowl, to hold the petals in position while the glue dries. You can also use plastilene effectively to hold the petals in interesting three-dimensional relationships while the epoxy dries.

Always use waxed paper under the glass when using epoxy glue to prevent adhering of the glass to the work surface.

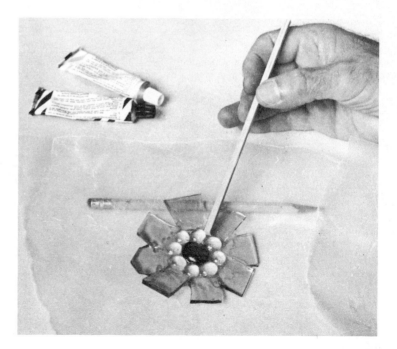

Little mounds of plastilene clay are useful for holding petals at a variety of angles.

Glue the ends of the petals together with drops of quick drying clear epoxy glue.

When the flowers and leaves are finished, fasten them to heavy-gauge wire cut in a variety of lengths. Flowers and leaves which are copper foiled can be soldered to the wire, while the epoxied flowers must be glued. The soldered areas, whether on the foil or on the wire, may be left silver or given a patina, as shown in earlier projects.

A vase which appears to be curved can be created by designing it as a series of tapered boxes which you copper-foil and solder together to give the impression of a curve. After assembling the vase, cut a piece of plastic foam to fit inside the bottom section. Now place the flowers into the vase, sticking the ends into the plastic foam to hold them in position. Make the arrangement as interesting as possible by placing the flowers at different heights and facing in different directions. Some flowers may be placed separately while others can be grouped together.

Cut out paper patterns with a mat knife and use them as a guide for cutting the glass pieces.

Laminated Stained Glass Panel in Light Box

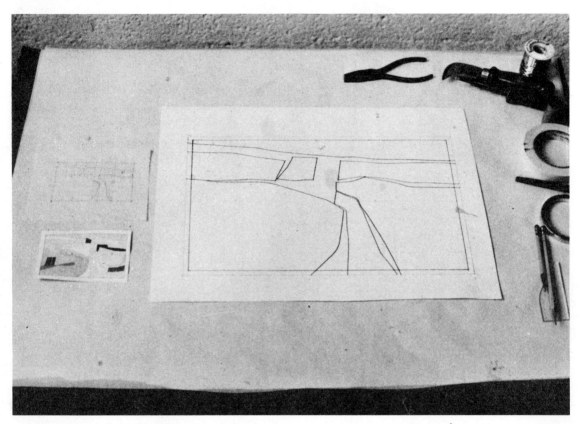

A good subject for a light glass panel is an abstract landscape design.

A practical and attractive solution to the problem of enjoying the beauties of stained glass after dark is to set a glass panel into a light box. This can be either a free-standing box that you can move from place to place or one set into a wall as a permanent feature.

A simplified abstract design based on landscape forms translated into stained glass becomes a rich focal point of color. Take any familiar scene and reduce the forms that you see into a few simplified planes. In the scene used here, several of the store fronts have been combined into one simple form.

Place the clear glass base over the design and brush epoxy glue over the area where the first glass piece is to be placed.

Concentrate on the silhouette rather than the detail of each form. As the glass panel will be done in two layers of transparent stained glass, you can overlap one form of the design over another.

Make several small sketches to scale, designing and redesigning until you are satisfied with the result. Use water color to wash in the various colors and, once again, experiment until you are satisfied. Now enlarge the scale sketch to full-size by using the squaring-off method. This simply means to divide both the sketch and the full-size drawing into equal squares, then copy each division from the small sketch onto the corresponding division of the full-size pattern.

Cut double-strength window glass as a base, allowing an additional $\frac{1}{2}$ inch beyond the edge of the design to allow space for setting the panel into the light box. Select a range of colors for the panel, bearing in mind that using one color of glass on

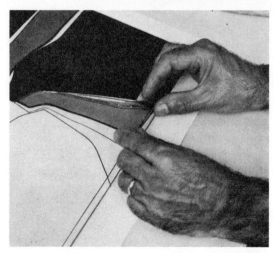

Press the correct glass piece down onto the area which has been covered with epoxy glue. Continue gluing pieces to the clear glass base until the first layer is complete.

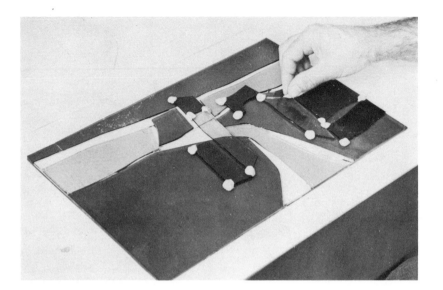

After cutting the glass pieces for the second layer, temporarily hold them in place with small bits of plastilene in order to judge the color relationships against the light.

Adjust color relationships if necessary before final gluing.

After any color changes have been made, be sure the glass is thoroughly cleaned before gluing the second layer. The transparency of stained glass creates a lovely interpenetration of forms and colors.

top of another gives the same effect as mixing paint. The panel shown was made of several different values of grey, tan, and off-white for the large main planes of the design, with stronger earth tones of russet and citron used for the smaller sections. Several of these overlap the large planes, creating interesting color mixtures.

Cut the large, main sections of stained glass over the full-size pattern. With the cut pieces of colored glass set aside, position the base piece of clear window glass over the full-size design. Brush clear epoxy glue over the area where the first piece of stained glass is to be placed and press the glass into place. Continue this procedure until all the pieces

of the first layer are glued to the clear glass. Use pieces of clear glass to fill in any areas not covered by stained glass.

Move on to cutting the pieces of glass for the second layer. Since you will want to judge the appearance of the second layer of glass before you glue it down, use small pieces of plastilene at the corners of each piece to hold them temporarily to the first layer. Hold the panel up to light to judge the effect of the color combinations. When you are satisfied with the relationships of the glass, remove the plastilene, clean the glass and glue the second layer in place as you did the first.

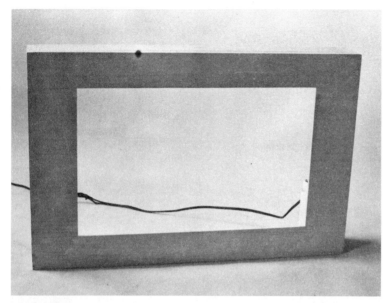

A glass panel set into an easily constructed light box will allow you to enjoy the beauty of stained glass after dark.

Light Box

Plan the dimensions of the light box to allow a space of at least 3 inches beyond the glass panel at both ends and a space of at least 2 inches at the top and the bottom of the panel. This will allow sufficient space to install the wiring and light fixtures.

Construct the box itself of plywood ½- to ¾-inch thick. Cut out the front opening with a coping saw or a jigsaw to the dimensions of the design portion of the glass panel. If you have a router, rabbet out an area inside the opening as wide as the border around the design. Otherwise, attach wood strips around the inside of the opening to support the glass panel when it is in place.

When you have cut the side pieces of the box to the proper dimension, nail and glue them to the face piece. Screw some simple electrical sockets to each of the bottom inside corners. Attach wires to the two sockets. If you are not experienced with wiring, be sure to seek expert advice. Use tall, thin 40-watt bulbs to provide illumination. Paint the inside of the box including the back piece with white paint so that it will distribute the light evenly. To prevent heat build-up inside the box when the lights are on, bore a series of holes at the top of the back piece. Also fasten aluminum foil to the inside corners behind the bulbs to reflect the light.

Place the glass panel into the opening, securing it with small nails. Attach the back piece using screws instead of nails so that you can remove it easily if you have to replace a bulb.

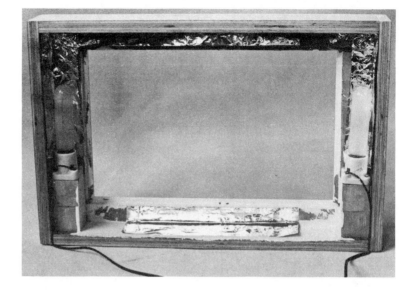

Lining the inside of the box with aluminum foil helps to distribute the light evenly.

Use small brads to fasten the panel in place.

93

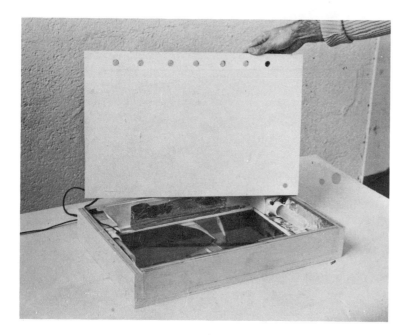

Drill a series of holes at the top of the back piece to ventilate the box and prevent overheating.

Paint the exterior of the light box in a neutral tone to set off the glowing colors of the finished laminated glass panel.

Index

Sources of Glass Supplies and Equipment

A free catalog of materials and equipment is available by mail from Whittemore-Durgin Glass Co., Box 2065 AB, Hanover, Mass. 02339.

In the United States

Acme Glass Co.
2215 W. Roosevelt Rd.
Chicago, IL 60608

Arts & Crafts Studio
7120 Little River Turnpike
Annandale, VA 22003

S.A. Bendheim Co., Inc.
122 Hudson St.
New York, NY 10013

Franklin Art Glass Studios
222 E. Sycamore St.
Columbus, OH 43206

Glass Masters Guild
621 Avenue of the Americas
New York, NY 10011

Glass Work Bench
159 Main St.
Flemington, NJ 08822

Glass Work Bench
107 S. Main St.
New Hope, PA 18938

Light Brigade Glassworks
378 E. Campbell Ave.
Campbell, CA 95008

Nervo Studios
650 University Ave.
Berkeley, CA 94710

Northwest Art Glass
904 Elliott Ave. W.
Seattle, WA 98119

Stained Glass Studio
12306 Lake City Way N.E.
Seattle, WA 98125

Whittemore-Durgin Glass Co.
Box 2065
Hanover, MA 02339

In England

Berlyne-Bailey and Company Ltd.
29 Smedley Lane
Cheetham, Manchester M8 8XB

The Pot Shop
8 Shillingford Street
Islington, London N1